Beauty

Beauty

A Collection of Poems to Empower African American Females to Redefine Personal Beauty Standards

Keishann Corley

BMcTALKS Press
4980 South Alma School Road
Suite 2-493
Chandler, Arizona 85248

Volume pricing is available to bulk orders placed by corporations, associations, and others. For details, please contact BMcTALKS Press at info@bmtpress.com

FIRST EDITION

Library of Congress Control Number: 2020918188

ISBN: 978-1-953315-02-1 (paperback)
ISBN: 978-1-953315-03-8 (eBook)

POETRY / American / African American & Black
POETRY / Women Authors

Cover and interior design by Medlar Publishing Solutions Pvt Ltd., India.
Cover inspired by sketch created by Keishann Corley.

Printed in the United States of America.

Dedication

For everyone

Introduction

Simple thoughts and words; ideas about beauty and my identity. All poems were written between 2019 and 2020. They chronicle personal experiences.

I do not mean to be offensive or rude. These are my truths.

Table of Contents

Background

As an African American woman, it is challenging navigating life and understanding the entanglement of compromise. Sometimes it feels like a double-edged sword: there are consequences when I fight, and consequences when I choose not to fight.

The Game

I don't have to be silenced in my words,
but I must choose my battles wisely.
I don't have to smile to be heard,
but I must speak at the right timing.

I don't have to wear my hair in a bun,
but I must understand how you see me.
I don't have to be on a strategic run,
but I must satisfy you completely.

I don't have to persuade you of what I am not,
but it is essential for me to try.
I don't have to fight for an open spot,
but this is the way I must oblige.

I don't have to reach for the galaxy,
but if I don't I might only reach the ground.
I don't have to hide the intelligence inside me,
but if I don't you'll find a way to pull me down.

I don't have to question how to approach you,
but if I don't you'll never hear me.
I don't have to pretend that I like you,
but if I don't I'll pay a substantial fee.

What Are Your Truths?

_____

_____

_____

_____

_____

_____

_____

_____

_____

_____

_____

_____

_____

_____

_____

_____

_____

_____

_____

_____

_____

_____

_____

Background

Someone once told me that makeup would enhance my looks, as if my looks required an enhancement. Many people wear makeup for different reasons. Some hide their freckles, blemishes, or acne. Some create a whole new look. Regardless of their choices, I decide to wear a natural appearance, which is more beautiful than anything that makeup can do. An image can be bought, but not beauty.

You Are Beautiful

You are beautiful
and
Makeup doesn't add to it.
Weave can't improve it.
Eyelashes are overrated.
Your natural beauty is the true statement.

It is witnessed in your smile.
Felt from your hugs.
Heard in your voice.
Recognizing your beauty is your choice.

It is not about jewelry.
It is not about clothes.
It is not about new shoes.
Your beauty simply glows.

Tattoos won't perfect it.
Piercings don't change it.
Rings can't make it shine brighter.
Your beauty is a natural highlighter.

So what you don't dance!
So what you don't sing!
Your talent is your talent.
And your beauty is the original thing.

Money cannot produce it.
Success cannot create it.
Exercise will not make it show.
Your beauty simply glows.

What Are Your Truths?

_____

_____

_____

_____

_____

_____

_____

_____

_____

_____

_____

_____

_____

_____

_____

_____

_____

_____

_____

_____

_____

_____

_____

Background

I did not always like my hair. It took a while to get used to it. It took more time to ignore the random comments people made or the looks people gave. The perception is I should perm it or get locs or slick my edges down with gel. My perception is I will do what I want and walk boldly and confidently with the beautiful grade of hair that rests perfectly on my head.

My Hair

is it a crime for me to like my hair?
why do I always feel attacked?
as if I must defend my beauty
and get you off my back.

I like the *poofiness* of my hair.
I love that it is black.
it may not always stay in place
but it is my hair and that's that.

sometimes it gets tangled.
sometimes I don't know what to do.
but it is still my hair and I love it
more than the thought of impressing you.

What Are Your Truths?

_____

_____

_____

_____

_____

_____

_____

_____

_____

_____

_____

_____

_____

_____

_____

_____

_____

_____

_____

_____

_____

_____

_____

Background

From being bullied as a kid to being bullied as an adult through microaggression and implicit biases, I learned to encourage myself and look beyond these oppressive experiences. This meant focusing on me and dropping things that stopped progress. Why live for the moment when I can build toward the future and live for a lifetime? No more pressure of trying to fit in because trends die, and legacies live forever. I am not a trend nor a popular fad; I am legacy fighting for my destiny.

My Question

You ever question the questioner?
Question the bully?
Question society and simply ask what for?
Why?

You ever tell them you don't want to?
You ever tell them you don't care.
Or it ain't worth it. I have!

I have because when I look at society, I see trouble.
I see lies; people living double lives because
of fear but it is over now.

I am tired and I have tried to be tired, but
I am really tired of trying to be me,
when the real me is me.

The real me that speaks and breathes.
The real me that cries (I try not to lie).
The real me that sees opportunity, a
chance to succeed;

Not by money, not by fame,
by my story and by my name.
By story, by name, by things I share and
tell the world.

The youth world.
Our teen world.
The world with our boys and our girls.

The world where I used to live but I
escaped and made it to reality, and my
reality is real.

My reality makes me feel like I can do it.
Reality that reminds me it's hard
work, long nights, teary eyes, chest pain but,
a never dying will.

A struggle.
A fight.
A choice to make it right to
reach back and say,
"No, my child, come up out of this world."

So I try with all my might to reach,
to feel, to write this unemotionally
but emotions are there.
Does it make me weak?

Does it make me weak when I stand up and say,

> "No, world … my money is mine." No artificials,
> fake nails, sacrificed hair to a God I don't serve,
> butt shots that intravenously attack nerves, breast
> growth surgeries, braces, whitening teeth that was
> never meant to be, abs as fake and thighs and butt
> to shake for a non-confident, low self-esteem man
> or woman living a generational cursed dream. I am
> done. All the marketed fun kills me. Drinking dete-
> riorates my body. Smoking destroys me, my meat,
> my cells, my already screwed-up, cannot-stop-
> thinking-get-these-spiders-outof-my-head-brain-
> cells and loosens my memory. So, "No world, you
> are not me!"

When I speak, I speak truth.
Sometimes it's in a disguise, but underneath it
all is heart, goodness, hope, love.

Love to reach for the little me
inside the little you, to pull
the little you inside the big me.

To welcome you to my world
embracing, encouraging a life-changing
destiny if you want it to be.

What Are Your Truths?

_____

_____

_____

_____

_____

_____

_____

_____

_____

_____

_____

_____

_____

_____

_____

_____

_____

_____

_____

_____

_____

_____

Background

A former coworker said, "Oh, Keishann, you would look so beautiful in a wig." My response was, "I am beautiful." It seems like women are brainwashed and say things to other females that individuals have said to them—insensible song lyrics and ideas about women that make no sense. I do not have to be made-up to be considered beautiful nor do I have to wear revealing clothing. My body is not a show for everyone to enjoy or comment on as if my beauty can be rated.

You Mad

Yeah, you mad cause I like my skirts
Past my knees, not tight so you know what
Can breathe. Nothing clinging to my skin that
Would make it hard to walk in my professional
Shoes that you roll your eyes at and have a
Problem with too.

Yeah, you mad without cause. Laughing at
My skin as if the only trend is to hide
Behind foundation, mascara, and color blends.
Tell me when black skin wasn't beautiful enough
To take in. Can't you see the vibrant melanin?
So what I have imperfections? My blemishes are me.
They are a part of my natural beauty.

Yeah, you mad and I heard what you said
Because you prefer fake hair and threads
Don't mean I'm lying in the same bed of
Synthetics that tear at my edges. As a babe
In college I learned my lesson . . .
My real hair is the authentic blessing.
"Oh, but you would look so beautiful with a wig."
As if you did? Wait, no offense
If you do because there is room for
Beauty in every *do*, but don't

Assume I desired to be groomed
By falsehood
Because what I understood to be true
And what I want to share with you is our hair
Is more beautiful than any fake do.

Yeah, you mad and I used to be
Used to feel like why am I being bullied?
You're black just the same as me but
Unfortunately, society blinded our eyes to
Love unconditionally to African American glory
So hear my plea. You do you
And let me do me.

What Are Your Truths?

_____

_____

_____

_____

_____

_____

_____

_____

_____

_____

_____

_____

_____

_____

_____

_____

_____

_____

_____

_____

Background

There is a story on YouTube about a woman who started getting butt injections at age twenty-two. Several years later she said, "I want people to see me more as [me]." What price do girls pay to create a different image of themselves? Then, as they age, they regret the choices they made.

Your Beauty

I'm not beautiful to
you because I
don't wear
makeup.

So make me
up. Make me your
definition of
beauty.

Teach me how to
perm my
hair. Straight
is beautiful
to you.

Lead me to
long extensions.
Braids
that tug
at my edges.

Once they're gone, teach
me about gel to
hide the bald spaces.

Recreate my
hairline. Is toxic
thickening spray
cool?

Once I've
mastered your methods, I'll
show my child what to
do.

Her hair isn't worth my
blessing. It must be
covered up.

I'll
teach her about makeup,
to hide, mask, and
cover up.

Her bare skin isn't good
enough. It's not beauty
alone.

She needs
mascara, and
lashes about an
inch long.

I will not
forget gel polish and artificial
Nails.

Everything you
taught about
beauty is all that I'll
tell.

I'll sell her
Lies about large
Butts and thick thighs.

Inject her
Body to disguise the
Original curvature.

Yeah, it would be
Wise to be known as
An asset, oversexualized
Through the eyes of society.

Let's play Russian
roulette with her
Perfect body.

What Are Your Truths?

_____

_____

_____

_____

_____

_____

_____

_____

_____

_____

_____

_____

_____

_____

_____

_____

_____

_____

_____

_____

_____

_____

Background

Instead of shaking what my momma gave me, I choose to shake my voice. There is power in words, in prayer, in uplifting and encouraging one another. There is beauty in everything about black women and girls, especially our intellect.

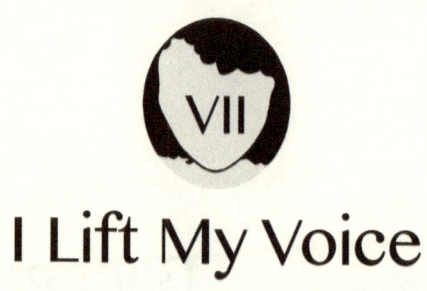

I Lift My Voice

I am lifting my voice.

No choice for the voiceless woman with inner conflicts; prejudices against a race that don't accept her for who she is.

I am lifting my voice.

Saying no, shouting no, to the cover, the liars, the hiders who peek behind clouds of artificially made beauty.

Esteem stricken from beneath the black woman's means.
She entered this world clean but the dangers of masking leave some passing up the queendom in exchange for gangrene.

In all her glory, she is the real thing, the wave that others are riding who try to buy into a likeness, trying to bite this but can't quite find it because it is black genes.

What I am saying is beauty reigns in us and we lay it down for deceitful maskings, inappropriate clothing, permanent marks that scar the natural covering that others try to obtain.

They are medically paying to be what we physically are. It is themselves they are trying to escape, so who is more fake?

I am lifting my voice.

A decision I run with holding true to the glue that connects me with you. Black beauty that exudes beyond the curvature of our hips, fullness in the lips, vibrant skin tones, strong bones, tightly coiled hair, stubborn minds that can produce any thoughts imagined there, but what do we choose?

Do we let the young black girl absorb the abuse? Do we laugh at the modest chick who let skirts go past her knees, the woman who avoids no sleeves, the athlete who always run with a T-shirt on?

I choose to shake the voice my momma gave me.

Use the mind to think and stand against enslaving behaviors that degrade me and the beauty God gave me naturally.

Shake the voice God gave you.

Awaken your mind to what you were born to. Lift your voice and choose to shine through the blackness on you, the resilient brilliance that lives in your genes will never go away.

What Are Your Truths?

_____

_____

_____

_____

_____

_____

_____

_____

_____

_____

_____

_____

_____

_____

_____

_____

_____

_____

_____

_____

_____

_____

Background

Ideas portrayed in some of the cartoons/movies our children watch can influence how they see themselves. I hope my nephew continues to enjoy reading with no shame. I hope he becomes the scientist he desires to be and not become worried about social pressures often chronicled in coming-of-age movies.

What Is Beauty?

What is beauty?

Is it makeup?
Is it jewelry?

Do my clothes make a difference?
Do my shoes have to be new?

Must I have straight teeth?
Must I compare myself to you?

The you on TV and all the
yous in the world.

Who push these
unbelievable images

and

force them on
our boys and our girls.

Our men and our
women are wrapped
in grief

with constant
thoughts and sour
belief that turns
their children's innocence
into an
ideal that stinks.

Where the
girl is too big,
the boy not buff enough.

The teens reading
books need to
smoke and drink stuff.

The loner must
be social, the virgin
needs sex.

Bully or be
bullied, join in with the
rest.

Join in this
mess beating
down pride

burning self-esteem,
which buries creativity
and murders my dreams.

What am I rising
for?

What do I stand
on,

when those
who identify as black

beat me with these false
standards, rip my identity,
leaving it torn.

What is beauty?

Is it a butt?
Is it thick thighs?

Is it big breasts?
Is it brown eyes?

Must I be slim?
Must I have abs?

Should I wear acrylic?
Should I wear a mask?

My body is not defining.
My hair is not bad.

I don't have to show cleavage.
I don't have to show my . . . rear end.

I listen to music for
content, read to learn words,
exercise to relieve stress, sleep
when life hurts.

What is beauty?
What is physical success?
What is this oppressive thinking?
it sounds like a mess.

What Are Your Truths?

_____

_____

_____

_____

_____

_____

_____

_____

_____

_____

_____

_____

_____

_____

_____

_____

_____

_____

_____

_____

Background

Even as an adult, older women have questioned my beauty in all its naturalness. Saying things like "Why don't you dress like a real girl?" I did not understand the question because everything on me is real—my hair, nails, eyelashes, physical attributes—it is all real. I questioned if *real* was still a thing in a world where you can decorate yourself into anything you want to be.

Real Again

I don't want to accept the
lashes, and I don't want to accept the
fake hair.
I don't want to accept the
makeup because my skin is good
enough to wear.

I don't want my edges to fall
out, and I don't want to get glue in my
eye.
I don't want my nails to
be weak and yellow. I don't want to
be stained with these lies.

My teeth are not the
straightest, and my skin is not the
clearest.
But I know that I am
beautiful even though I
don't always hear it.

At times I wonder . . .
Where is our confidence?
Where is our esteem?
Where is the admiration for natural
beauty, not these artificial things?

All of these synthetics and all of
these cover-ups.
These damaging acrylics, these
expensive butt shots and tummy tucks.

Haven't we seen? Do we
recognize that this is too much?
Let us encourage our
children, tell them not to
lose their natural touch.

What Are Your Truths?

_____

_____

_____

_____

_____

_____

_____

_____

_____

_____

_____

_____

_____

_____

_____

_____

_____

_____

_____

_____

_____

Background

To my niece, Keilani Corley (The Babe): Already at the age of six, I can see that you feel it. The feeling that you are not enough, of being the other, of being ashamed of your color, ashamed of your hair, but Babe, you are beautiful. You are enough. Your hair is thick and curly. It is just as beautiful as you are.

You Are Beautiful

You are beauty.
A princess not drawn.
A wonderful, colorful girl
Who was and is loved since you were born.
Even before you arrived,
The angels gazed in awe of you.
Your hair, skin tone, and eyes,
Like Jesus in the womb.
Let me tell you who you are.
Do not absorb social lies.
The rankings of beauty there
Are a false, horrible disguise.
Realize how strong you are.
Your ability to fly is not a dream.
Think big and pray large.
You are beautiful.
You don't need artificial markings.

What Are Your Truths?

_____

_____

_____

_____

_____

_____

_____

_____

_____

_____

_____

_____

_____

_____

_____

_____

_____

_____

_____

_____

_____

_____

_____

Background

As I was reading about the elements of the policymaking system, I came across a term called, *black* box. It is defined as any system, model, or theory that operates without explaining how the system produces inputs into outputs. Why, in all the words available in the English language, did someone use the word *black* to describe this process that seems to be unknown? This is one small example of how views are embedded historically in American culture.

Black

I hate that I am aware of the word *Black*.
Every time I see it, *Black*. This word that
is used to described dirt, and fear, and things that are unclear,
things unknown, darkness, scariness; and then, I
have to check a box to agree with that?
I am not this *Black*!
This black that rests in the minds of three-year-olds
the darkness of Ursula, the hue of supervillains,
the complexion of the princess's maid.
TV is throwing shade at me and expects
my niece to grow up and believe that
she is not pretty, but we
are not this version of *Black*.

What Are Your Truths?

_____

_____

_____

_____

_____

_____

_____

_____

_____

_____

_____

_____

_____

_____

_____

_____

_____

_____

_____

_____

_____

_____

Background

This poem was written in response to those affected by the following social media post.

> "For a while now, I have felt like Ringmaster of the ****show. Today has done me in! I do not want to be ringmaster, someone come get the monkeys and all the circus friends."

Monkey is culturally insensitive. Everyone may not know it; however, this is an example of the reinforcement of the symbols in society about how we are viewed. I cannot speak to the intentions of the writer. I simply want humans—particularly those who identify as African American or Black—to know that you are more than this.

XII

You Will

When I look at you, I do not see a monkey.
I do not see a beast.
I see untapped potential that will not rise because of cultural defeat.

Do not let the heat of slavery beat your dreams.
You are bigger and more than what they can ever think.

Imagine how the history books tried to erase you.
Imagine stories of Kings and Queens who look just like you.

I need you to imagine and pull strength from who you are.
Mathematicians, scientists, doctors, and experts on overcoming
      life's scars.

Let go of the image that shows the impoverished black man.
Let go of the thoughts of failure. Get up and rise again.

Use your story to breathe out the pain.
Share your successes. Write your goals. Make your ideas plain.

Rise for the occasion and learn the game.

Learn the rules to use the tools that will
pull wealth to you.

Forgive the bullies, the racists, and all the prejudiced behaviors too.
Stand on a humane character who continues to love no matter what
    they do.

Be a keeper of your word and always follow through.
Search the depths of your mind and throw away insane statements
    that
are not true about you

because

You will succeed.
You will accomplish your dreams.
You will work toward destiny.
You will get an education or a college degree.
You will speak up and protect the weak.
You will overcome doubt and self-defeat.
You will encourage your brother and sister genuinely.
You will overcome the pressures of society.
You will focus and become whatever you desire to be.

What Are Your Truths?

_____

_____

_____

_____

_____

_____

_____

_____

_____

_____

_____

_____

_____

_____

_____

_____

_____

_____

_____

_____

www.ingramcontent.com/pod-product-compliance
Lightning Source LLC
Chambersburg PA
CBHW031257120626
46545CB00007B/2863